A is for Aloha

2ND EDITION

Stephanie Feeney
Eva Moravcik

Photographs by
Jeff Reese

A LATITUDE 20 BOOK
UNIVERSITY OF HAWAI'I PRESS
HONOLULU

Printed in China
23 22 21 20 19 18   6 5 4 3 2 1

Library of Congress Cataloging-in-Publication Data
Names: Feeney, Stephanie, author. | Moravcik, Eva,
    author. | Reese, Jeff, photographer (expression)
Title: A is for aloha / Stephanie Feeney and
    Eva Moravcik ; photographs by Jeff Reese.
Description: 2nd edition. | Honolulu : University of
    Hawaiʻi Press, [2018] | "A latitude 20 book."
Identifiers: LCCN 2017054877 | ISBN
    9780824876548 (cloth alk. paper)
Subjects: LCSH: English language—Alphabet—
    Juvenile literature. | Alphabet. | Vocabulary. |
    Hawaii—Juvenile literature. | Hawaii—Social life
    and customs—Juvenile literature. | Alphabet books.
Classification: LCC PE1155 .F4 2018 |
    DDC 421/.1—dc23
LC record available at https://lccn.loc.gov/2017054877

University of Hawaiʻi Press books are printed
on acid-free paper and meet the guidelines for
permanence and durability of the Council on
Library Resources.

Designed by Mardee Melton

About the Book

A **IS FOR ALOHA** uses an alphabet-book format to portray some of the people, places, plants, animals, and activities that make up the everyday life of children in Hawai'i. The first edition was created in 1980, to give Hawai'i's young children a book illustrating familiar experiences that were relevant to them. It was also intended to give children in other places a glimpse of what life is like on our beautiful islands and to convey the spirit of *aloha* to people everywhere.

A is for Aloha has been enjoyed by children in Hawai'i for more than thirty-five years. They have enjoyed seeing images of people who look like them and their families. This second edition is intended to revisit the spirit of the first. The beautiful new photographs taken by Jeff Reese reflect island children's lives today and show the brilliant colors that characterize the Hawaiian Islands. The authors and photographer are delighted to introduce the new color version of this groundbreaking book.

WE WISH TO ACKNOWLEDGE the children who were the subjects of these photographs, the teachers and directors who were so helpful and generous with their time, and the families who allowed us to use images of their children in this book. We also appreciate the patience and cooperation of the children and staff of Leeward Community Center Children's Center. Special thanks to teachers Jackie Rabang and Steve Bobilin. Mahalo nui loa to Kumu Hula Miki'ala M. Kanekoa and the children and families of Halau 'O Kaululaua'e. Thanks also to Mamie Lawrence Gallagher and the children at Mo'o School in Honolulu, Hawai'i.

We are profoundly grateful to Kona and Ed Matautia and their children for their participation in this project. Thanks also to Desiree Rabang, Aria Andrade, Sandra Bassett, Kanalu and Adan Asam, Keano Davis, Sherry Nolte, Georgia Acevedo, Philip Moravcik, and Don Mickey. We also wish to express our appreciation to the Waikīkī Aquarium and to Suzi Mechler and the Kailua Canoe Club.

Stephanie Feeney
Portland, Oregon

Eva Moravcik
Honolulu, Hawai'i

Aa

Bb

Cc

A a

aloha

Bb

ball

beach

boy

Cc

canoe

Dd

Daddy

egret

Ff

friend

Gg

gecko

Hh

hula

li

island

Jj

jump

Kk

kite

Ll

lei

Mm

Mommy

N n

noodles

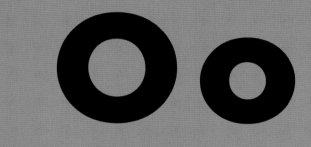

octopus

Pp

plumeria

parrot

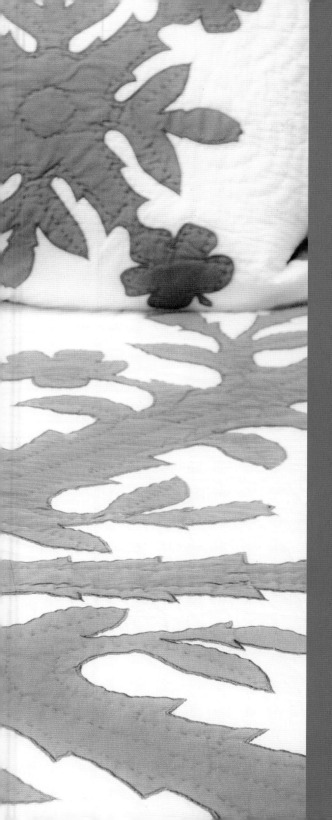

Qq

quilt

Rr

rain

Ss

surf

surfboard

surfer

Tt

tūtū

Uu

ʻukulele

Vv

volcano

Ww

waterfall

Xx

X-ing

Yy

yucky

Zz

zori

About Hawai‘i

THE STATE OF HAWAI‘I is composed of a chain of islands in the Pacific Ocean. It is very different from the rest of the United States, referred to in Hawai‘i as "the mainland." In Hawai‘i, the weather is warm all year long and the sky is usually blue. The ocean can appear turquoise and is so clear that you can see coral reefs and tropical fish. The green mountains of Hawai‘i were created by volcanoes, though most no longer erupt. There are still two active volcanoes on the island of Hawai‘i, the biggest island. There are many kinds of trees, lush tropical plants, and brightly colored flowers, like hibiscus, bird of paradise, and ginger, that bloom all year long. Lizards, birds, and mongooses live in Hawai‘i, but there are no snakes or squirrels. When it rains and the sun is shining, you can see beautiful rainbows.

The first settlers of Hawai‘i were Polynesians, who came by canoe from far-distant islands in the Pacific. Many years after the Polynesians arrived, missionaries and whalers came from the eastern United States. Europeans came to trade. Later, people from Asia and the Pacific, including Japanese, Chinese, Filipinos, Koreans, Vietnamese, Samoans, and Micronesians, came to live and work in Hawai‘i. The people who came to Hawai‘i from these places brought their own plants, animals, arts and crafts, household items, and customs. Hawai‘i is an interesting and colorful place to live and visit because so many peoples and cultures live here together.

The lives of children in Hawai‘i are in most ways like the lives of children everywhere. They live in houses or apartments in the city (the biggest is Honolulu on the island of O‘ahu) or in the country. They get from place to place by car and bus and between islands by plane. Children live with their mothers and fathers and sometimes with grandparents (called *tūtū** by many island children) and other relatives. Most people in Hawai‘i speak English, and many speak and understand a rhythmic, shortened form of English called "pidgin" that includes words from Hawaiian and other languages spoken in Hawai‘i.

---

* Because the Hawaiian language does not distinguish between singular and plural with an *s* at the end of a word, the proper way to say the plural form of *tūtū* is just "*tūtū.*"

Children in Hawai'i like to do the things that children do everywhere. They go to school, play with their friends, help out at home, listen to stories, watch television, and play games. Because it is usually warm and sunny and beaches surround the islands, children also enjoy many activities near the ocean. They like to swim, dig in the sand and build sand castles, go fishing with their families, and sometimes go for rides in canoes or on surfboards.

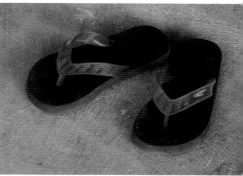

Most of the time children wear shorts, T-shirts, and sandals. In most homes it is not considered polite to wear shoes in the house, so people leave them by the door before they go inside. Women and girls sometimes wear long, brightly colored dresses called *mu'umu'u,* and men and boys sometimes wear colorful Hawaiian-patterned *aloha* shirts. Children in Hawai'i never need snowsuits, mittens, or boots, because it is never cold enough to snow except at the top of the tallest mountains.

Foods that children on the mainland like to eat—hamburgers, hot dogs, pizza, milk, and ice cream—are also enjoyed by children in Hawai'i. They like a noodle soup called *saimin,* rice wrapped in seaweed called *musubi,* and "shave ice"—cones of shaved ice with flavored syrup. They also enjoy Chinese, Japanese, Korean, Filipino, and Hawaiian foods and tropical fruits such as pineapples, papayas, mangoes, lychees, and coconuts. Many people in Hawai'i eat rice with most of their meals. A scoop of rice is often served with eggs at breakfast.

The holidays of Halloween, Thanksgiving, Christmas, Valentine's Day, and Easter are celebrated in Hawai'i, as they are on the mainland. Holidays from other places are also celebrated here. Children enjoy firecrackers and a special dance called the "lion dance" on Chinese New Year. Japanese Boys' Day is marked by hanging up a fish banner for each boy in a family and Girls' Day with the displaying of beautiful Japanese dolls. The birthdays of Hawaiian Prince Kūhiō and King Kamehameha are state holidays. In Hawai'i, May Day is called Lei Day. It is a time when children in school wear flower *lei* and sing songs and dance dances from the various cultures of Hawai'i.

Another way in which Hawai'i differs from the rest of the United States is that it is the only state that once had kings and queens. Today Hawai'i has a government like the other states, but people still remember the days of the monarchy. Beautiful songs written about the kings and queens of Hawai'i are still sung, and the much-loved song *Aloha 'Oe* was written by Hawai'i's last queen, Lili'uokalani.

If you want to learn more about our lovely islands, there are many books available in your local library, and online, about the history, geography, and cultures of Hawai'i.

Xx

Yy

Zz

About the Words

Aloha

Aloha is a Hawaiian word that conveys warm feelings and can be used to say "hello," "goodbye," and "I love you." When people in Hawai'i are kind and compassionate, they are said to be showing *aloha*.

Hula

Hula is a Hawaiian dance that tells a story sung in a chant or song *(mele)*. *Hula* is an honored part of Hawaiian culture. Many children in Hawai'i learn to dance *hula* in a *hula* school *(hālau)* from a *hula* teacher *(kumu hula)*.

Canoe

A Hawaiian canoe is a narrow boat fitted with outriggers (side supports that prevent tipping) and is moved with paddles. Ancient Hawaiians traveled between islands in outrigger canoes, and paddling them is still a popular sport.

Lei

Lei is the Hawaiian word for a garland of flowers, leaves, shells, or feathers. *Lei* are given on special occasions, along with a kiss, to show affection or appreciation. They can be worn around the neck, on the head, or around the brim of a hat.

Egret

An egret is a large white bird in the heron family. Cattle egrets are often seen in Hawai'i eating the bugs that are disturbed when grass is mowed and flying together to roost as evening falls.

Octopus

An octopus is a large-headed, soft-bodied, ocean-dwelling animal that has eight arms covered with suckers. In Hawai'i octopuses are caught by spear on the coral reefs and used for food.

Gecko

The gold dust day gecko is a small species found in Hawai'i. This green gecko with colorful markings lives in trees in the rainforest and feeds on insects, fruit, and nectar. It is seen increasingly often in homes and gardens in Hawai'i.

Parrot

Different kinds of parrots live in the wild in Hawai'i. The parrot you see here is a rose-ringed, or ring-necked, parakeet. Parrots are gregarious birds with a loud squawking call and are found on the islands of O'ahu, Maui, and Kaua'i. Though they live in the wild today, parrots are not native to Hawai'i.

Plumeria

A plumeria is a flower that grows on a tree. It grows almost everywhere in Hawai'i. Plumeria trees have large waxy leaves and clusters of delicate, fragrant flowers that are used to make *lei*. The trees have no leaves from December to March and bloom in spring and summer.

Volcano

A volcano is an opening in the earth's surface from which molten rock called lava erupts. The islands of Hawai'i were once volcanoes, and most of the land on the islands is formed from lava rock.

Quilt

Hawaiian quilts have distinctive large, appliquéd, symmetrical designs based on island flowers and plants and usually have only two colors. Hawaiians learned to make quilts from early missionaries. Each quilt takes many hours to create, and they are treasured by families.

Zori

Zori is the Japanese word for a thonged sandal with an open back. *Zori* are popular in Hawai'i, where people often refer to them as "slippers."

Tūtū

Tūtū is the Hawaiian word for grandparent. Formally, a grandmother is a *tūtū wahine* and a grandfather is a *tūtū kāne*, but many children in Hawai'i just call a beloved grandparent their *tūtū*.

'Ukulele

An *'ukulele* is a small, usually four-stringed, guitar-like instrument that was introduced to Hawai'i by the Portuguese, though its name is Hawaiian. It is a popular instrument in Hawai'i, often made of beautiful koa wood from trees that grow there.

Sharing This Book with Children

SHARING A PICTURE BOOK with a child is a very special experience. Whether you live in the islands or faraway, *A is for Aloha* is a way to share the beauty of Hawai'i with your child. As you look at the pictures and read together you will be helping your child to enjoy books—an important part of learning to read.

While *A is for Aloha* is not intended to teach reading, it can be used to help develop some early literacy skills. First and foremost it can stimulate language. Children need to enjoy words and talking before they start to read. Begin by looking at the pictures with your child, talk about what each of you sees, and make a connection to your child's life (*The boy is holding a red ball. It's like your red ball!*). Talk with each other about your feelings and reactions (*Would you like to ride in a canoe? I think it would be fun*). If your child wants to know more, share some of the information from the sections about Hawai'i and about the words (*It says here that there are wild parrots in Hawai'i*).

If your child seems interested, talk about the letters and the sounds the letters make. Children who notice similarities between the big letters on the page and the little letters in the words describing the pictures are showing you that they may be interested in learning about letters. Understanding that letters are associated with sounds is important in learning to read.

You can help your child learn some letter sounds by pointing to a letter (for example, *d*), saying the sound (*d-d-d-d*), and then saying the word (*daddy*), emphasizing the initial sound. If your child seems interested, talk about other words that begin with the same sound (*dog, duck, dig*). Be playful and keep it fun. It is easier and more effective to begin with consonants that always make the same sounds rather than with vowels, which make many different sounds. Teaching the sounds the letters make, rather than memorizing the alphabet, is a better way to help a child learn to read. If your child doesn't seem to understand or be interested in the sounds of letters, don't worry. The most important thing is to enjoy the book together. Go back to talking about the pictures and try again in a few weeks or months.

Remember, the most valuable thing you can do is to have a relaxed, pleasant experience sharing the book. We created this book for children, parents, and teachers to enjoy! We hope it will enrich the time you spend together.

Aloha,
Stephanie and Eva

About the Authors

STEPHANIE FEENEY is professor emerita of education at the University of Hawai'i, where she taught and administered early childhood education programs for many years. She has written extensively about the field of early education and is the author of three other children's books published by University of Hawai'i Press. The first edition of *A is for Aloha*, published in 1980, grew out of her concern that there were no available books relevant to the lives of young children in Hawai'i.

EVA MORAVCIK is professor of early childhood education at Honolulu Community College and coordinator of the Leeward Community College Children's Center. She has been a preschool teacher and early childhood program director in Hawai'i for many years. In collaboration with Stephanie, she is the author of two textbooks for teachers of young children. She has been teacher and aunty to most of the beautiful children you see in the pages of this book and is married to its photographer, Jeff Reese.

About the Photographer

JEFF REESE was the photographer for the University of Hawai'i Press book *Hawaii is a Rainbow* and two early childhood education textbooks authored by Stephanie and Eva. He also contributed many of the photos in *Sun and Rain: Exploring Seasons in Hawai'i*. Jeff currently works in Oregon as an education specialist for the Coast Guard and alternates his time between Hawai'i and the Oregon coast. He appreciates the unique beauty of Hawai'i and its children and is a great admirer of the work of Hella Hammid, whose black-and-white photos were featured in the first edition of this book.